TAE KWON-DO

Grading Syllabus
WHITE BELT TO BLACK BELT

The Official Tae Kwon-Do Association of
Great Britain training manual

Produced by the Senior Instructors of the TAGB

KTP Promotions

Introduction
This publication is intended to give students studying Tae Kwon-Do a comprehensive guide to Korean Terminology and associated techniques. It is not intended to replace regular training with a qualified instructor in a dojang.
We hope this book will make the learning of Korean terminology easier and become an invaluable reference manual for all students of Tae Kwon-Do.

ISBN 978-0-9560652-0-9

Note
Whilst every effort has been made to ensure that the content of this book is as technically accurate as possible, neither the authors nor the publishers can accept responsibility for any injury or loss sustained as a result of the use of this material.

Acknowledgments
Thanks to the research of the T.A.G.B council for their help in producing this book.
Photographs: Slyvio Dokov @ Lifestyle Photography.
Editing: Keith O'Neill & Liz Read.
Design & Typeset: Paul Harding.
Thanks to Master Ron Sergiew 8th Dan & Mr Terry Read 5th Dan for Demonstrating.

For more information about this publication
Contact:
Tae Kwon-Do International Ltd
PO Box 1937
Southam
CV47 1ZY
Tel: 01926 810333

First Published 2008, Reprinted 2014
Copyright © 2014 by Tae Kwon-Do International
Published by KTP Promotions

A Brief history of the T.A.G.B.

Tae Kwon-Do's popularity was well established world wide by 1983, however political differences within Korea and within the two world governing bodies, the International Tae Kwon-Do Federation (ITF) and the World Tae Kwon-Do Federation (WTF) led to internal disagreements and threatened to tear the world of Tae Kwon-Do apart. Several attempts were made to unite the two Tae Kwon-Do organisations, but these were unsuccessful.

It was largely due to this that in August 1983 it was decided to form, in the UK, an organisation that would be run on principles, far more democratic than were permitted by the two fore mentioned groups. This became the basis of the Tae Kwon-Do Association of Great Britain (TAGB)

Five years later, in April 1988, the TAGB became a founder member of the British Tae Kwon-Do Council (BTC). The BTC is the only Tae Kwon-Do body recognised by the United Kingdom Sports Council and incorporates 13 different organisations and represent 45,000 plus Tae Kwon-Do practitioners.

The TAGB, with over 25,000 members represents the next stage in the evolution of Tae Kwon-Do. With its grounding in the ethos and tenets which were first adopted by the Hwa Rang over 2,000 years ago and its open acceptance and constant development of patterns, training techniques and ideas, it stands poised to take the ancient fighting form and make it a martial art for the 21st century, successfully linking the distant past with an equally distant, and certainly no less wondrous future.

In view of this, in 1993, a new world body was formed called Tae Kwon-Do International. The new body encompasses both ITF and WTF stylists, it is entirely non-political in orientation and its sole aim is to promote the benefits of Tae Kwon-Do as a sport and as a martial art worldwide. The TAGB is a founding member of this new organisation.

Key Dates Summary

21st August 1983	T.A.G.B formed.
21st April 1988	B.T.C formed.
13th November 1993	Tae Kwon-Do International formed.

TAGB COMMITTEE MEMBERS

Gianni Peros
Committee Member

Brian Towndrow
Committee Member

Ron Sergiew
Treasurer

Michael Dew
Vice Chairman

Kenny Walton
English National Coach

Don Atkins
Secretary

Paul Donnelly
Liaison Officer

David Oliver
Chairman

T.A.G.B. AREAS

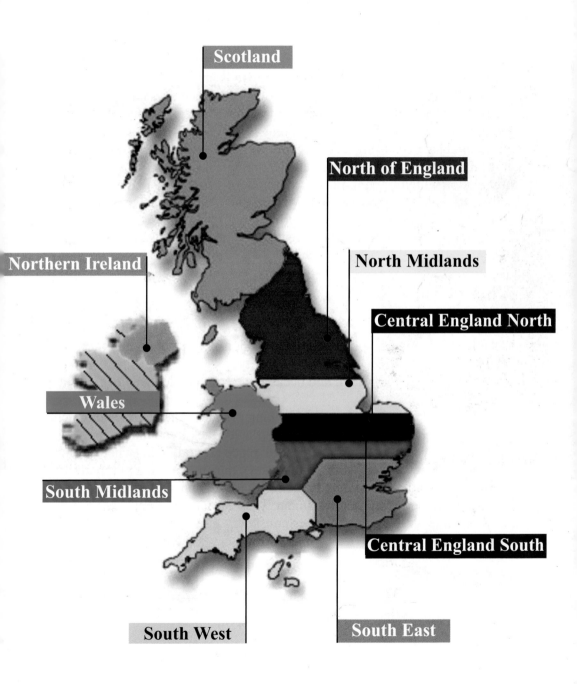

Scotland

North of England

North Midlands

Central England North

Northern Ireland

Wales

South Midlands

Central England South

South West

South East

A brief history of Tae Kwon-Do

Tae Kwon-Do is an ancient form of unarmed combat practiced for many centuries in Korea. It became perfected in its present form by Major General Choi Hong Hi (1918 - 2002), and has been scientifically developed and modernised since its introduction to the world on **11th April 1955.** Translated from Korean, **Tae** means to jump, kick or smash with the foot, **Kwon** means to punch, strike or destroy with the hand and **Do** is art, method or way. It is proven to be the most powerful system of self defence ever devised. To the Korean people Tae Kwon-Do is more than a mere use of skilled movements. It also promotes a way of life with a strong sway towards the more philosophical side, particularly instilling a concept and spirit of self imposed discipline and an ideal of noble moral re-armament. In these days of violence and intimidation which seem to plague our modern societies, Tae Kwon-Do enables the weak to possess a fine weapon to defend themselves and when strongly applied it can be very dangerous.

Tae Kwon-Do was introduced to Great Britain in **1967** by Rhee Ki Ha.

What is Taek Kyon?

Taekyon, or Taek kyon is a traditional Korean martial art, stemming from Soobak, which was first practiced in Korea during the Koguryo Dynasty (37 BC - AD 668).

It spread to the Silla kingdom and became the bare handed way of fighting of the Hwarang.

At the height of its popularity even the king practiced taek kyon and matches were frequent. However, the next king outlawed taek kyon matches, disillusioned by the gambling which took place around them (where people would gamble away their wives and houses), thus making it a purely military art. Soobak eventually separated into different segments - grappling, kicking, etc. Taek kyon being one such segment. Taek kyon movements are very fluid and dance-like with the practitioners constantly moving. It does not have the hard snap kicks of Tae Kwon-Do but a softer way of generating power.

Ancient & Modern depictions of Taek kyon.

General Choi Hong Hi

General Choi Hong-Hi, born 9th November 1918; 15th June 2002.
Born in what is now North Korea when it was under Japanese occupation, Choi fled to Japan to complete his education after a wrestler was set on his trail following a gambling dispute. In 1942, he was drafted into the Japanese army, but was imprisoned for attempting to escape to join the opposition Korean Liberation Army in 1945. Only the liberation of Korea saved him from the death penalty.

After the war, the division of Korea between north and south left him unable to return to the land of his birth. He rose quickly in the new South Korean army and, two years after the outbreak of the Korean war in 1950, he created an officer training program and an infantry division that provided Tae Kwon-Do instructors.

After the cessation of hostilities in 1953 his rise continued, and in 1961 he supported the military coup d'etat, but suffered a setback when General Park Chung-Hee emerged as the new president. In the late 1940s, Park had received a death sentence, later rescinded, from a military panel that had included Choi, who was thus forced to retire from the military following the coup.

In 1962, he was sent to Malaysia as ambassador, but after his return to South Korea in 1965 he continued to find life under the Park regime so intolerable that in 1972 he left for Canada. Choi took the headquarters of the ITF to Toronto with him, and South Korea responded by forming a new organisation, the World Taekwondo Federation (WTF), based in Seoul.

Choi's final years were marked by his efforts to return to North Korea. He introduced Tae Kwon-Do there in 1980.

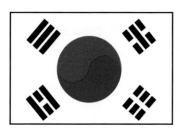

Korean Flag

Tae Kwon-Do Oath

As a student of Tae Kwon-Do, I do solemnly pledge to abide by the rules and regulations of the Tae Kwon-Do Association, to strive always to be modest, courteous and respectful to all members, in particular my seniors, to put the art into use only for self defence or defence of the weak and never to abuse my knowledge of the art.

Key Dates Summary

11th April 1955   Tae Kwon-Do inaugurated.
2nd July 1967   Tae Kwon-Do introduced to Great Britain.

Rules & Regulations

Dojang
The dojang is where we come to train in the art of Tae Kwon-Do, and as such it must be respected: by adhering to the following etiquette you help create an environment conducive to learning of Tae Kwon-Do:

Bow when entering or leaving the dojang.

Remove shoes while in the dojang.

There is to be no food or drink within the dojang.

Do not chew gum while in the dojang.

Do not swear, or use offensive language while in the dojnag.

NEVER use negative or defiant body language while in the dojang (i.e. Standing with your hands on your hips, or with your arms folded over your chest).

Do not argue, or lose self control while in the dojang.

Do not throw things, such as kicking paddles, in the dojang - when passing anything from one student to another, you should do so while bowing.

It is every student's responsibility to help maintain the cleanliness of the dojang.

Dobok
The Tae Kwon-Do uniform is not only practical, but symbolic of purity a readiness to be taught: a consistency in appearance reminds us that we are all students of the same martial art:

All students should wear a dobok to class, which should be well maintained, clean and unwrinkled.

Dobok's should be adjusted to fit properly. The rolling up of sleeves and trousers is unacceptable.

No jewellery is to be worn during training.

Long hair must be tied back.

Finger and toe nails must be kept trimmed.

If you must adjust your uniform, turn to the back of the dojang and away from the instructor to do so.

Bowing
Bowing is a means of showing respect: it is never inappropriate to bow, but these are the circumstances when it is prudent to:

Bow when entering or leaving the dojang.

Bow at the beginning and ending of class.

Bow when you first see, and again when you depart from your instructor, your instructor's instructors, and any black belts.

Bow to any higher ranking student who has assisted you in your training.

Bow to your opponent before and after sparring.

Bow when shaking hands with any student or instructor.

Bow when passing things (such as kicking paddles) to another student.

Respect

Aside from bowing, here are some other ways to demonstrate respect for your instructor, and fellow students:

Address all black belts and instructors by their last names or sir / ma'am, students are required to know their instructors titles.

When being addressed by the instructor:

Stand to attention, answer with yes sir / ma'am, speak loudly.

When the conversation is complete, bow to the instructor.

Higher ranking students should show leadership by assisting lower ranking students whenever necessary - lower ranking students should show their appreciation by demonstrating their respect and following the same etiquette they would for an instructor.

Lower ranking students should show respect for higher ranking students by holding doors open so that they may enter the dojang first.

Students should volunteer to assist the instructor whenever possible (i.e. carrying equipment, setting up for events, cleaning the dojang, etc.).

Line up in order (facing the front of the dojang, highest to lowest, right to left, front to back). Students should not walk through the rows.

Students should wait to break from line-up until the highest ranking student has done so.

Training

Students should always come to class ready to put forth their greatest effort to train; the following etiquette helps demonstrate that the student has the proper mind-set for Tae Kwon-Do training:

Move quickly to line-up.

Ki'hap loudly during training.

Do not engage in unnecessary talking or movements which are distracting to other students and disrespectful to the instructor.

Students shall not engage in sparring without the permission of the instructor.

You should always ask permission from the instructor before leaving the dojang during class.

If you arrive late to class, stand at attention to let the instructor know you are ready to join class (the instructor will incorporate you into the line-up as soon as it is convenient to do so).

If you forget your belt, take your place in the line-up at the very back of class (regardless of your rank / grade).

Inform the instructor if you will be absent.

Students should inform the instructor before the class when they have a temporary injury or illness that may affect their performance during the lesson. Any permanent conditions should have been disclosed on their membership form.

Never come to a Tae Kwon-Do class or event under the influence of alcohol or drugs - you will be permanently dismissed from the club if you do so.

Grading Etiquette

A grading is the students method of progressing through the Tae Kwon-Do belt system. Within the TAGB all gradings are carried out by the founder members and committee members, all of whom have vast experience in Tae Kwon-Do and will expect the highest standards in order to allow you to advance.

In tradition with the military history of Tae Kwon-Do, gradings are conducted in a formal manner. Detailed below are items of etiquette to assist a student in successfully passing the gradings:

Ensure your dobok is clean and pressed.

Make sure your belt is tied correctly.

The date and location of your grading should be filled out correctly in the appropriate place in your licence booklet.

If you are required to spar as part of your grading, you will need a full set of undamaged and clean TAGB approved safety equipment.

Arrive in plenty of time for the start of your grading.

Address all senior grades and instructors as Sir or Ma'am.

When entering the grading dojang be sure to bow towards the front of the dojang or the flags (if present).

When your name is called answer loud and clear with "Here Sir" or "Here Ma'am".

Make your way quickly to your starting mark as instructed.

When at your mark take up attention stance, bow and then ready stance.

When asked for name and grade, come to attention, raise your right hand and loudly say your name and present grade, then assume ready stance again.

Listen to instruction from your examiner and at no time talk unnecessarily. Should you need to adjust your dobok or belt, do so while facing away from your examiner.

When answering theory questions you will be asked to come to attention, bow then assume ready stance. You may change position only to demonstrate techniques or stances if requested to do so.

Only when dismissed by the examiner may you leave your mark.

Your grading begins when you enter the grading dojang and is only finished when you are instructed to leave the dojang.

When leaving the dojang be sure to bow towards the examiner and / or the flags.

Tenets of Tae Kwon-Do
(Tae Kwon-Do Jungshin)

Courtesy
Ye Ui

To be polite to your instructors, seniors and fellow students.

Integrity
Yom Chi

To be honest with yourself. You must be able to define right from wrong.

Perseverance
In Nae

To achieve a goal, whether it is a higher grade or any technique, you must not stop trying; you must persevere.

Self Control
Guk Gi

To lose your temper when performing techniques against an opponent can be very dangerous and shows lack of control. To be able to live, work and train within your capability shows good self control.

Indomitable Spirit
Baekjul Boolgool

To show courage; when you and your principles are pitted against overwhelming odds.

Tae Kwon-Do Patterns

What is a pattern?

A set of fundamental movements, mainly defence and attack, set in a logical sequence against one or more imaginary opponents.

Why do we perform patterns?

To learn sparring techniques, stances, correct facing, improve facing, improve posture, focus movements, body shifting, breath control, muscle toning, learn to relax and tense muscles at the correct time and practice other techniques that are not possible in other areas of training.

Why do we learn the interpretations of patterns?

Pattern interpretations are derived from people and events in Korean history and show one or more of the tenets to give us inspiration.

Why are there 24 patterns?

The reason there are 24 patterns in Tae Kwon-Do is because the founder, Major General Choi Hong Hi, compared the life of a man with a day in the life of the Earth, and believed that some people should strive to bequeath a good spiritual legacy to coming generations and in doing so gain immortality. Therefore, if we can leave something behind for the welfare of mankind, maybe it will be the most important thing to happen in our lives, as the founder says:

> "Here I leave Tae Kwon-Do for mankind.
> As a trace of a man of the late 20th century
> The 24 patterns, one day or all of my life".

Can you explain the theory of power?

Reaction Force
Pulling the opposite arm back in co-ordination with the strike creates a reaction force.
Concentration
Applying impact force onto the smallest target area.
Equilibrium
Use reaction arm for dynamic stability to keep the body balanced.
Breath Control
Tense abdomen to breathe out on impact. See why do we ki'hap on page 14.
Mass
Use hip twist and knee spring to increase body weight.
Speed
The most essential factor for power, however all the other factors contribute to speed.

The following points should be considered when performing patterns:-

1   Patterns should begin and end on the same spot.
        This will indicate the performers accuracy.

2   Correct posture and facing must be maintained at all times.

3   Muscles of the body should be tensed or relaxed at the
        appropriate moments in the exercise.

4   The exercise should be performed in a rhythmic movement with
        absence of stiffness.

5   Each pattern should be accelerated or decelerated according to
        instructions.

6   Each pattern should be perfected before moving on to the next.

7   Students should know the purpose of each movement.

8   Students should perform each movement with realism.

Start positions for colour belt patterns

Chon Ji   Won Hyo   Joon Gun   Hwa Rang
Dan Gun   Toi Gye
Do San
Yul Gok
Choong Moo

Commands & Numbers

Commands

Attention	**Charyot**
Bow	**Kyong-Ye**
Ready	**Junbi**
Shout	**Kihap**
Start / Begin	**Si-Jak**
Stop	**Goman**
Return to Ready	**Barrol**
Dismiss	**Haessan**
Forward	**Apro Kaggi**
Backward	**Dwiyro Kaggi**
About Turn	**Dwiyro Torro**
Left	**Wen**
Right	**Orun**
Inward	**Anaero**
Outward	**Bakaero**
Break	**Hechyo**
Press Ups	**Momtong Bachia**
Training Hall	**Dojang**
Training Suit	**Dobok**
Belt	**Ti**
Pattern	**Tul**
Instructor	**Sabum**
Student	**Jeja**

Numbers

One	**Hanna**
Two	**Dool**
Three	**Set**
Four	**Net**
Five	**Dasaul**
Six	**Yosaul**
Seven	**Ilgop**
Eight	**Yodoll**
Nine	**Ahop**
Ten	**Yoll**

Why do we kihap?

Correct breath control will not only improve ones stamina and speed, but will also focus the power of a technique. Correct breathing in martial arts is performed using the diaphragm. A sharp exhaling of breath during movement, with a sudden stop on impact of technique tenses the abdomen and maximizes power and effort of delivery. The breathing technique used in Tae Kwon-Do is called kihap or shout. Although called a shout, be careful not to use the vocal cords instead of the diaphragm, otherwise all the benefits will be lost.

Getting Started

Attention Stance
Charyot Sogi
50 - 50
Weight distribution
Heels together

Bow
Kyong Ye
Bend 15 degrees
Look forward

1 Shoulder Width

Parallel Ready
Stance
Narani Junbi Sogi
50 - 50
Weight distribution

Key to pattern abbreviations

W	Walking Stance	VS	Vertical Stance
L	L Stance	C	Closed Stance
S	Sitting Stance	X	X Stance
F	Fixed Stance	SLOW	Slow Motion
BRS	Bending Ready Stance	FAST	Fast Motion
RFS	Rear Foot Stance	CONT	Continuous Motion
LOW	Low Stance		

White Belt Terminology

White belt signifies innocence, having no previous knowledge of Tae Kwon-Do.

What do the words **Tae**, **Kwon** & **Do** Mean?
Foot (Tae), Hand (Kwon) & Way or Art (Do)

Where did Tae Kwon-Do originate? **South Korea**

High Section   **Nopunde**
Middle Section   **Kaunde**
Low Section   **Najunde**

What is Korean for training hall?   **Dojang**
What is Korean for training suit?   **Dobok**
What is Korean for belt?   **Ti**

What is the Korean for stance?   **Sogi**

What are the five Tenets of Tae Kwon-Do?
Courtesy
Integrity
Perseverance
Self Control
Indomitable Spirit
See Page 11 for more details on Tenets.

Name of your instructor(s) _____   _____

Instructors grade   _____   _____

50 - 50
Weight distribution

1½ Shoulder widths long
between big toes.

Walking Stance
Gunnun Sogi

1 Shoulder width wide
between centre of insteps.

Walking Ready Stance
Gunnun Junbi Sogi

Sitting Stance
Annun Sogi

50 - 50
Weight distribution

1½ Shoulder widths wide
between big toes.

Block   **Makgi**

Blocking

Tae Kwon-Do blocks are designed to defend against a range of techniques, from different directions and using a variety of attacking tools or weapons. Blocks will either smash/destroy or deflect/deviate the attacking tool.

Outer Forearm Low Block
Bakat Palmok Najunde Makgi
Blocking Tool: Outer Forearm

Knuckles level with shoulder

Inner Forearm Middle Block
An Palmok Kaunde Makgi
Blocking Tool: Inner Forearm

Rising Kick
Ap Cha Olligi

Rising kick is used as a training kick, designed to develop the muscles used in a wide range of kicks. This exercise also improves hip mobility and flexibility.

Ensure the exercise is begun in Walking Ready Stance, the rising leg is kept straight throughout the entire movement and then returned to the walking stance position after the kick.

Obverse Punch	**Baro Jirugi**
Reverse Punch	**Bandae Jirugi**
4 Directional Punch	**Saju Jirugi**

Inner Forearm	**An Palmok**
Outer Forearm	**Bakat Palmok**

19

4 Directional Punch No.1

Begin: Parallel Ready Stance
Left arm in punch position

1 Step forward in right walking stance, perform right middle punch.
   Turn left 90° into left walking stance, perform left outer forearm low block.
2 Step forward in right walking stance, perform right middle punch.
   Turn left 90° into left walking stance, perform left outer forearm low block.
3 Step forward in right walking stance, perform right middle punch.
   Turn left 90° into left walking stance, perform left outer forearm low block.
4 Step forward in right walking stance, perform right middle punch with a kihap
   Turn left 90° and bring right leg up to parallel ready stance, leave right arm in
   punch position.

1 Step forward in left walking stance, perform left middle punch.
   Turn right 90° into right walking stance, perform right outer forearm low block
2 Step forward in left walking stance, perform left middle punch.
   Turn right 90° into right walking stance, perform right outer forearm low block
3 Step forward in left walking stance, perform left middle punch.
   Turn right 90° into right walking stance, perform right outer forearm low block
4 Step forward in left walking stance, perform left middle punch with a kihap.

Saju Jirugi No.1

4 Directional Punch No.2

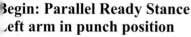

Begin: Parallel Ready Stance
Left arm in punch position

1 Step forward in right walking stance, perform right middle punch.
  Turn left 90° into left walking stance, perform left inner forearm middle block.
2 Step forward in right walking stance, perform right middle punch.
  Turn left 90° into left walking stance, perform left inner forearm middle block.
3 Step forward in right walking stance, perform right middle punch.
  Turn left 90° into left walking stance, perform left inner forearm middle block.
4 Step forward in right walking stance, perform right middle punch with a kihap.
  Turn left 90° and bring right leg up to parallel ready stance, leave right arm in
  punch position.

1 Step forward in left walking stance, perform left middle punch.
  Turn right 90° into right walking stance, perform right inner forearm middle block.
2 Step forward in left walking stance, perform left middle punch.
  Turn right 90° into right walking stance, perform right inner forearm middle block.
3 Step forward in left walking stance, perform left middle punch.
  Turn right 90° into right walking stance, perform right inner forearm middle block.
4 Step forward in left walking stance, perform left middle punch with a kihap.

Saju Jirugi No.2

Yellow Tag Terminology

Yellow belt signifies the earth from which the plant sprouts and takes root as the foundations of Tae Kwon-Do are laid.

What is a pattern?

A set of fundamental movements, mainly in defence and attack, set in a logical sequence against one or more imaginary opponents.

What is the Korean for pattern?   **Tul**

70 - 30
Weight distribution

1½ Shoulder widths long between rear foot sword and front toes.

L Stance
Niunja Sogi

Forearm Guarding Block
Palmok Daebi Makgi
Blocking Tool: Outer Forearm

Walking Stance   **Gunnun Sogi**
Walking Ready Stance   **Gunnun Junbi Sogi**

22

Forearm Rising Block
Palmok Chookyo Makgi
Blocking Tool: Outer Forearm

Why is the fist higher than the elbow in rising block?
To deflect the attack.

Double Punch
Doo Jirugi

Obverse Punch
Baro Jirugi
Strike Tool: Fore Fist
Target Area: Solar Plexus

Reverse Punch
Bandae Jirugi
Strike Tool: Fore Fist
Target Area: Solar Plexus

Front Kick
Ap Chagi
Strike Tool: Ball of Foot

Knife Hand Strike
Sonkal Taerigi
Strike Tool: Knife Hand
Target Area: Neck / Philtrum

Step Turn	**Omgyo Didimyo Dolgi**
Ball of Foot	**Ap Kumchi**
Knife Hand	**Sonkal**
Fore Fist	**Ap Joomuk**

19 Movements

Chon Ji means literally "Heaven and Earth." In the Orient it is interpreted as the creation of the world, or the beginning of human history. Therefore, it is the initial pattern performed by the beginner. The pattern consists of two similar parts - one to represent Heaven and the other the Earth.

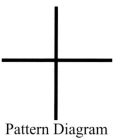

Pattern Diagram

Begin: Parallel Ready Stance

	Technique	Section	Stance	Direction
1	Outer Forearm Block	Low	W	Turn Left 90°
2	Obverse Punch	Middle	W	Forward
3	Outer Forearm Block	Low	W	Turn Right 180°
4	Obverse Punch	Middle	W	Forward
5	Outer Forearm Block	Low	W	Turn Left 90°
6	Obverse Punch	Middle	W	Forward
7	Outer Forearm Block	Low	W	Turn Right 180°
8	Obverse Punch	Middle	W	Forward
9	Inner Forearm Block	Middle	L	Turn Left 90°
10	Obverse Punch	Middle	W	Forward
11	Inner Forearm Block	Middle	L	Turn Right 180°
12	Obverse Punch	Middle	W	Forward
13	Inner Forearm Block	Middle	L	Turn Left 90°
14	Obverse Punch	Middle	W	Forward
15	Inner Forearm Block	Middle	L	Turn Right 180°
16	Obverse Punch	Middle	W	Forward
17	Obverse Punch	Middle	W	Forward
18	Obverse Punch	Middle	W	Backward
19	Obverse Punch	Middle	W	Backward

Chon Ji Tul

25

Yellow Belt Terminology

Yellow belt signifies the earth from which the plant sprouts and takes root as the foundations of Tae Kwon-Do are laid.

What is Korean for 3 step sparring?	**Sambo Matsoki**
Why do we do 3 step sparring?	**Focus, Distance & Timing**

L Stance	**Niunja Sogi**
Walking Stance	**Gunnun Sogi**
Parallel Ready Stance	**Narani Junbi Sogi**

Knife Hand Guarding Block
Sonkal Daebi Makgi
Blocking Tool: Knife Hand

Twin Outer Forearm Block
Sang Bakat Palmok Makgi
Blocking Tool: Outer Forearms

Outer Forearm Inward Block
Bakat Palmok Anaero Makgi
Blocking Tool: Outer Forearm

Back Fist Front Downward Strike
Dung Joomuk Ap Naeryo Taerigi
Strike Tool: Back Fist
Target Area: Nose

Front Kick

Chamber Position

Front Kick
Ap Chagi
Strike Tool: Ball of Foot

Front Snap Kick
Ap Cha Busigi
Strike Tool: Ball of Foot

Front Kick Foot Shape

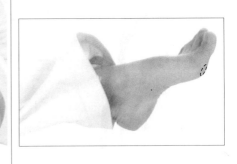

Front kick is executed using the ball of the foot. The foot should be pushed forward with the toes pulled back allowing the ball of the foot to strike the target.

Turning Kick

Chamber Position

Turning Kick
Dollyo Chagi
Strike Tool: Ball of foot

Turning Kick Foot Shape

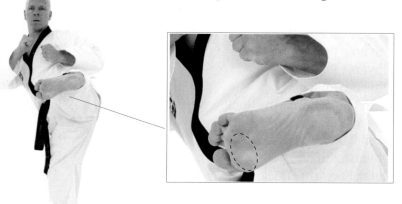

Turning kick is executed using the ball of the foot. The heel is higher than the toes, the toes are pulled back to allow the ball of the foot to strike the target.

21 Movements

Dan Gun is named after the Holy Dan Gun, the legendary founder of Korea who established the country in 2333BC.

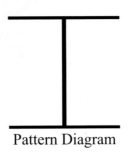

Pattern Diagram

Begin: Parallel Ready Stance

	Technique	Section	Stance	Direction
1	Knife Hand Guard Block	Middle	L	Left 90°
2	Obverse Punch	High	W	Forward
3	Knife Hand Guard Block	Middle	L	Right 180°
4	Obverse Punch	High	W	Forward
5	Outer Forearm Block	Low	W	Left 90°
6	Obverse Punch	High	W	Forward
7	Obverse Punch	High	W	Forward
8	Obverse Punch	High	W	Forward
9	Twin Outer Forearm Block	Mid / High	L	Left 270°
10	Obverse Punch	High	W	Forward
11	Twin Outer Forearm Block	Mid / High	L	Right 180°
12	Obverse Punch	High	W	Forward
13	Outer Forearm Block	Low	W	Left 90°
14	Rising Block	High	W	-
15	Rising Block	High	W	Forward
16	Rising Block	High	W	Forward
17	Rising Block	High	W	Forward
18	Knife Hand Strike	Middle	L	Left 270°
19	Obverse Punch	High	W	Forward
20	Knife Hand Strike	Middle	L	Right 180°
21	Obverse Punch	High	W	Forward

Dan Gun Tul

At 8th kup yellow belt students are introduced to both set sparring and free sparring.

Set sparring is a controlled, prearranged set of movements designed to help the student develop focus, distance and timing, and is used as a safe method to introduce self defence techniques and a prelude to free sparring.

Basic defensive techniques and skill are developed through 3 step sparring. Defending only against a simple punch, the complexity of the counter attack increases as the student advances.

Both attacking and defensive techniques and skills progress with the introduction of 2 step sparring at 5th kup blue tag belt. The complexity of attack and defence again increases as the student advances.

Semi free sparring introduces the element of unpredictability, the attacker is encouraged to add an element of realism, thus improving the defenders ability to deal with a real attack.

One step sparring is introduced from 3rd kup red tag belt onwards. The student is required to create their own set of defensive and counter attack sequences. This form of set sparring is more inline with self defence.

Free sparring is the final evolution of sparring, most clubs now introduce this element to students early on in their training, allowing the student to gain a greater understanding of the art and prepares the student for more advanced skills later in their development.

In order to comply with safety regulations a full set of TAGB approved safety equipment should be worn for free sparring.
See page 77 and your instructor for more details.

Focus	Distance	Timing
A means of control to effectively defend against incoming attacks and to respond with an accurate and speedy counter attack.	Correct distancing ensures defensive and attacking techniques are effective and that the exercise is carried out safely.	Timing is critical to the effective execution of both blocking and attacking techniques. Deflection and strikes are only effective if timed correctly.

Sambo Matsoki

The ready postition for 3 step sparring
This applies to all numbers 1 to 10

Measuring

To ensure correct distance is established at the beginning of 3 step sparring, the attacking student is advised to measure the distance between themselves and their opponent as demonstrated by their instructor.

Getting ready to attack & defend

Correct start position for the attacker is to perform a left arm low section outer forearm block in left walking stance (right leg back), then kihap to show attacker is ready to begin.

The attacker performs three middle section obverse punches, at a steady pace.

The defender starts in parallel ready stance, and kihaps when ready to defend.

For clarity, only the defence techniques have been listed overleaf.

Number 1

1

2

Left Walking Stance
Middle Section
Inner Forearm Block

Right Walking Stance
Middle Section
Inner Forearm Block

Counter Attack

3

Left Walking Stance
Middle Section
Inner Forearm Block

Left Walking Stance
Middle Section
Reverse Punch

The counter attack is executed by drawing back the the blocking arm and performing a middle section reverse punch towards the attackers solar plexus.

Number 2

1

Left L Stance
Middle Section
Inner Forearm Block

2

Right L Stance
Middle Section
Inner Forearm Block

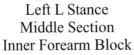

Left L Stance
Middle Section
Inner Forearm Block

Counter Attack

Left L Stance
High Section
Knife Hand Strike

The counter attack is executed by moving the rear leg to the left, then the front leg into an L stance to the outside of the opponent's front foot and then striking to the side of the opponent's neck, with right knife hand.

Number 3

Left L Stance
Middle Section
Outer Forearm Inward Block

Right L Stance
Middle Section
Outer Forearm Inward Block

Counter Attack

Left L Stance
Middle Section
Outer Forearm Inward Block

Left L Stance
Back Fist Front Strike

The counter attack is executed by drawing back the blocking arm and then sliding forward as if to strike the opponent on the bridge of the nose.

Number 4

1

Left L Stance
Middle Section
Inner Forearm Block

2

Right L Stance
Middle Section
Inner Forearm Block

3

Left L Stance
Middle Section
Inner Forearm Block

Number 4

Sitting Stance
Middle Section
Measure

Sitting Stance
Middle Section
Right Punch

Sitting Stance
Middle Section
Left Punch

The counter attack is executed by moving the rear leg to the left into a sitting stance. A measure is made with the left hand, followed by a double punch.

37

Green Tag Terminology

Green belt signifies the plants growth as the Tae Kwon-Do skills begin to develop.

What is Korean for 3 step sparring?   **Sambo Matsoki**

Why do we do three step sparring?   **Focus, Distance & Timing**
See Page 31 & 114.

What is Korean for release move?   **Jap Yasol Tae**

When was Tae Kwon-Do introduced to the UK?   **1967**

Outer Forearm Wedging Block
Bakat Palmok Hechyo Makgi
Blocking Tool: Outer Forearms

Knife Hand Outward Block
Sonkal Bakaero Makgi
Blocking Tool: Knife Hand

Outer Forearm High Block
Bakat Palmok Nopunde Makgi
Blocking Tool: Outer Forearm

39

Back Fist High Side Strike
Dung Joomuk Nopunde Yop Taerigi
Strike Tool: Back Fist
Target Area: Temple

Straight Fingertip Thrust
Son Sonkut Tulgi
Strike Tool: Fingertips
Target Area: Solar Plexus

1

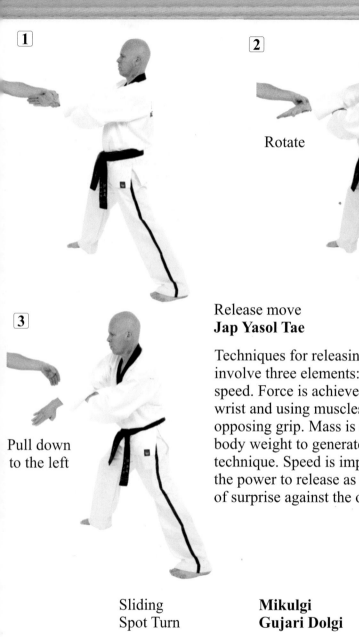

2

Rotate

Release move
Jap Yasol Tae

Techniques for releasing from all grabs
involve three elements: force, mass and
speed. Force is achieved by rotating the
wrist and using muscles to react against the
opposing grip. Mass is simply using your
body weight to generate extra power to the
technique. Speed is important to generate
the power to release as well as the element
of surprise against the opponent.

3

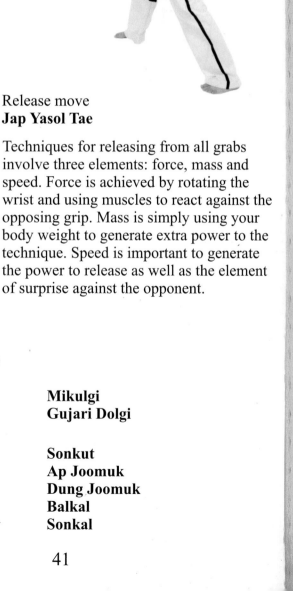

Pull down
to the left

Sliding	**Mikulgi**
Spot Turn	**Gujari Dolgi**
Fingertip	**Sonkut**
Fore Fist	**Ap Joomuk**
Back Fist	**Dung Joomuk**
Foot Sword	**Balkal**
Knife Hand	**Sonkal**

Side Kick

Side Kick
Yop Chagi
Strike Tool: Foot Sword

Side Kick Foot Shape

Side kick is executed using the foot sword.
The heel should be higher than the toes and
the edge of the foot pushed forward to strike
the target.

42

24 Movements

Do San is the pseudonym of the patriot Ahn Ch'ang Ho (1876 - 1938), who devoted his life to furthering the education of Korea and its independence movement.

Pattern Diagram

Begin: Parallel Ready Stance

	Technique	Section	Stance	Direction
1	Outer Forearm Block	High	W	Left 90°
2	Reverse Punch	Middle	W	-
3	Outer Forearm Block	High	W	Right 180°
4	Reverse Punch	Middle	W	-
5	Knife Hand Guarding Block	Middle	L	Left 90°
6	Straight Fingertip Thrust	Middle	W	Forward
7	Release Move			
	Back Fist Side Strike	High	W	Left 360°
8	Back Fist Side Strike	High	W	Forward
9	Outer Forearm Block	High	W	Left 270°
10	Reverse Punch	Middle	W	-
11	Outer Forearm Block	High	W	Right 180°
12	Reverse Punch	Middle	W	-
13	Wedging Block	High	W	Left 135°
14	Front Snap Kick	Middle	-	Forward
15	Obverse Punch	Middle	W	-
16	Reverse Punch	Middle	W	-
17	Wedging Block	High	W	Right 90°
18	Front Snap Kick	Middle	-	Forward
19	Obverse Punch	Middle	W	-
20	Reverse Punch	Middle	W	-
21	Rising Block	High	W	Left 45°
22	Rising Block	High	W	Forward
23	Knife Hand Strike	Middle	S	Left 270°
24	Knife Hand Strike		S	Foot to Foot (Right)

Do San Tul

Number 5

1

Right L Stance
Middle Section
Outer Forearm Block

2

Left L Stance
Middle Section
Outer Forearm Block

Counter Attack

Sitting Stance
High Section Punch
Outer Forearm Middle Block

The counter attack is executed by sliding the right leg into sitting stance and performing a middle section outer forearm block to the inside of the opponent's punching arm whilst simultaneously punching towards the opponent's jaw with the right fist.

Number 6

**Right L Stance
Middle Section
Knife Hand Block**

**Left L Stance
Middle Section
Knife Hand Block**

Counter Attack

**Sitting Stance
High Section Knife Hand Inward Strike
Knife Hand Middle Block**

The counter attack is executed by sliding the right leg into sitting stance and performing a middle section knife hand block to the inside of the opponent's punching arm whilst simultaneously executing an inward moving knife hand strike to the opponent's neck with the right knife hand.

Number 7

1

Right L Stance
Middle Section
Outer Forearm Block

2

Left L Stance
Middle Section
Outer Forearm Block

3

Right L Stance
Middle Section
Forearm Guarding Block

Right Leg
Middle Section
Front Kick

Walking Stance
Middle Section
Obverse Punch

Walking Stance
Middle Section
Reverse Punch

The counter attack is executed by sliding backwards on a right 45 degree
diagonal away from the opponent in forearm guarding block, performing a
right leg front kick followed by a double punch in walking stance. Both
attacks are aimed towards the opponents solar plexus.

47

Green Belt Terminology

Green belt signifies the plants growth as the Tae Kwon-Do skills begin to develop.

When was the TAGB formed?   **21st August 1983**

What is the target area for the reverse knife hand strike in No.10 three step sparring?
The side of the neck.

Why do you pull your hand back to your chest when performing inward moving knife hand strike in Won Hyo?
It acts as a reaction force and is also in a ready position to perform a block or strike. It can also be interpreted as grabbing your imaginary opponent to pull them towards the striking tool.

What is 3 step semi free sparring in Korean?
Ban Jayoo Matsoki

Why do we do 3 step semi free sparring?
Advanced techniques, closer to traditional free sparring. Focus, distance and timing play a more important role. See page 31 & 114.

1½ Shoulder widths long
between big toes.

Closed Ready Stance A
Moa Junbi Sogi A
50 - 50 weight distribution
Toes and heels touching.

Fixed Stance
Gojung Sogi
50 - 50 weight distribution
Feet at 90° to each other.

Bending Ready Stance
Guburyo Sogi
100% weight distribution on
standing leg.
Foot protects standing knee.

Bending ready stance is a transient position held for a brief moment as the knee is lifted ready to execute a kick.

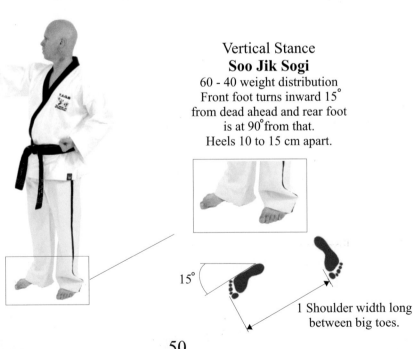

Vertical Stance
Soo Jik Sogi
60 - 40 weight distribution
Front foot turns inward 15°
from dead ahead and rear foot
is at 90° from that.
Heels 10 to 15 cm apart.

15°

1 Shoulder width long
between big toes.

Inner Forearm Circular Block
An Palmok Dollimyo Makgi
Blocking Tool: Inner Forearm

NOTE

Circular block can either be used to block two separate attacks, for example a front kick & middle section punch OR it can be used to scoop up a front kick to unbalance the opponent.

Outer Forearm Waist Block   Palm Inward Pushing Block
Bakat Palmok Hori Makgi   **Sonbadak Anaero Miro Makgi**
Blocking Tool: Outer Forearm   Blocking Tool: Palm

Knife Hand Inward Strike
Sonkal Anaero Taerigi
Strike Tool: Knife Hand
Target Area: Side of Neck

Side Punch
Yop Jirugi
Strike Tool: Fore Fist
Target Area: Solar Plexus

Reverse Knife Hand Strike
Sonkal Dung Taerigi
Strike Tool: Reverse Knife Hand
Target Area: Neck

Back Kick
Dwit Chagi
Strike Tool: Back Sole

Foot Shifting

Jajun Bal

Foot Sword
Back Sole
Ball of Foot
Palm
Reverse Knife Hand

Balkal
Dwi Kumchi
Ap Kumchi
Sonbadak
Sonkal Dung

52

28 Movements

Won Hyo is the name of the Silla Dynasty monk who reputedly introduced Zen Buddhism to Korea in AD 686.

Pattern Diagram

Begin: Closed Ready Stance 'A'

	Technique	Section	Stance	Direction
1	Twin Forearm Block	High / Mid	L	Left 90°
2	Inward Knife Hand Strike	High	L	-
3	Side Punch	Middle	F	Slip Left Foot Forward
4	Twin Forearm Block	High / Mid	L	Foot to Foot Right 180°
5	Inward Knife Hand Strike	High	L	-
6	Side Punch	Middle	F	Slip Right Foot Forward
7	Forearm Guarding Block	Middle	BRS	Left 90°
8	Side Piercing Kick	Middle	-	Forward
9	Knife Hand Guarding Block	Middle	L	-
10	Knife Hand Guarding Block	Middle	L	Forward
11	Knife Hand Guarding Block	Middle	L	Forward
12	Straight Fingertip Thrust	Middle	W	Forward
13	Twin Forearm Block	High / Mid	L	Left 270°
14	Inward Knife Hand Strike	High	L	-
15	Side Punch	Middle	F	Slip Left Foot Forward
16	Twin Forearm Block	High / Mid	L	Foot to Foot Right 180°
17	Inward Knife Hand Strike	High	L	-
18	Side Punch	Middle	F	Slip Right Foot Forward
19	Circular Block	Mid / Low	W	Left 90°/ Forward
20	Front Snap Kick	Low	-	Forward
21	Reverse Punch	Middle	W	-
22	Circular Block	Mid / Low	W	-
23	Front Snap Kick	Low	-	Forward
24	Reverse Punch	Middle	W	-
25	Forearm Guarding Block	Middle	BRS	Forward
26	Side Piercing Kick	Middle	-	On Left Leg
27	Forearm Guarding Block	Middle	L	Left 270°
28	Forearm Guarding Block	Middle	L	Foot to Foot Right 180°

Won Hyo Tul

Number 8

Right L Stance
Middle Section
Knife Hand Block

Left L Stance
Middle Section
Knife Hand Block

Right L Stance
Middle Section
Knife Hand Guarding Block

54

Right Leg
Middle Section
Side Kick

L Stance
High Section
Knife Hand Strike

CLOSE UP
High Section
Knife Hand Strike

The counter attack is executed by sliding backwards on a right 45 degree diagonal away from the opponent in knife hand guarding block. Perform a rear leg side kick towards the opponents solar plexus followed by a right knife hand strike in a left L stance towards the side of the opponents neck.

Number 9

Right L Stance
Middle Section
Palm Inward Pushing Block

Left L Stance
Middle Section
Palm Inward Pushing Block

Right L Stance
Middle Section
Palm Inward Pushing Block

Counter Attack

Right Leg
Middle Section
Turning Kick

Chamber Position
for High Section
Knife Hand Strike

Vertical Stance
High Section
Knife Hand Strike

The counter attack is executed by performing a middle section turning kick towards the opponents solar plexus, the spent foot is placed next to the opponents leading foot, drawing the rear foot up to form a vertical stance, striking the back of the opponents neck with a right knife hand strike.

Number 10

1

Right L Stance
Middle Section
Knife Hand Block

2

Left L Stance
Middle Section
Knife Hand Block

3

Right L Stance
Middle Section
Knife Hand Guarding Block

Counter Attack

Chamber Position
for Middle Section
Reverse Side Kick

Right Leg
Middle Section
Reverse Side Kick

Walking Stance
High Section
Reverse Knife Hand Strike

The counter attack is executed by sliding backwards on a right 45 degree diagonal away from the opponent in a knife hand guarding block. Perform a reverse side kick with the right leg to the opponents solar plexus followed by reverse knife hand strike with the left hand in right walking stance towards the side of the opponents neck.

Ban Jayoo Matsoki
(Basic)

3 Step semi free sparring (Basic Level) introduces the student to a more realistic form of set sparring.

All attacks are known and performed in a safe and controlled manner to allow the student to learn the correct focus, distance and timing associated with this form of set sparring.

Attacker

The attacker begins in forearm guarding block in a right L stance.
The attacker will perform three kicks in the following order:-

Front kick
Side kick
Turning kick

All kicks should be aimed to the middle section.

Defender

The defender blocks each kick with a waist block.
The counter attack is a reverse punch toward the attackers solar plexus.

Defender and attacker then change roles and repeat until requested to stop.

Students should kihap to notify each other that both are ready to begin. The defending student also kihaps on the counter attack.

1

Front Kick   L Stance
Waist Block

2

Side Kick   L Stance
Waist Block

3

Turning Kick   L Stance
Waist Block

Counter Attack

Reverse Punch
to solar plexus

Blue Tag Belt Terminology

Blue belt signifies the Heaven, towards which the plant matures into a towering tree as training in Tae Kwon-Do progresses.

When was the BTC formed?   **21st April 1988**

What is Korean for 2 step sparring?   **Ibo Matsoki**

What is the difference between 3 step and 2 step sparring?
2 step sparring requires a more complex combination of techniques in defence and attack, therefore greater emphasis on focus, distance and timing is required.
See Page 31 & 114.

What is Korean for free sparring?   **Jayoo Matsoki**

X Stance	Back Fist High Side Strike
Kyocha Sogi	**Dung Joomuk Nopunde Yop Taerigi**
Majority of weight on the standing foot.	Strike Tool: Back Fist
	Target Area: Temple

X Fist Pressing Block
Kyocha Joomuk Noollo Makgi
Blocking Tool: Back of Forearms

Palm Upward Block
Sonbadak Ollyo Makgi
Blocking Tool: Palm

Double Forearm Block
Doo Palmok Makgi
Blocking Tool: Inner Forearm

What is the purpose of the
rear arm in this block?
1. Reinforcing the lead arm
2. Reaction
3. Act as a guard
4. Positioned to block

Hooking block can turn into a grasping block by wrapping the fingers around the opponents wrist.

Start position for hooking block

Grasping Block
Butjuba Makgi

Palm Hooking Block
Sonbadak Golcho Makgi
Blocking Tool: Palm

Twin Knife Hand Block
Sang Sonkal Makgi
Blocking Tool: Knife Hand

Outer Forearm Waist Block
Bakat Palmok Hori Makgi
Blocking Tool: Outer Forearm

NOTE
The open hand is used
as a focus point.

Elbow Front Strike
Palkup Ap Taerigi
Strike Tool: Elbow
Target Area: Solar Plexus

Twin Upset Punch
Sang Dwijibo Jirugi
Strike Tool: Fore Fist
Target Area: Kidneys

Flat Fingertip Thrust
Opun Sonkut Tulgi
Strike Tool: Fingertips
Target Area: Eyes / Neck / Philtrum

Twin Vertical Punch
Sang Sewo Jirugi
Strike Tool: Fore Fist
Target Area: Cheekbones

Knee Kick
Moorup Chagi
Strike Tool: Knee
Target Area: Groin / Solar plexus

Side Elbow Thrust	**Yop Palkup Tulgi**
Back Fist Side Strike	**Dung Joomuk Yop Taerigi**
Side Punch	**Yop Jirugi**
Reverse Turning Kick	**Bandae Dollyo Chagi**
Front Snap Kick	**Ap Cha Busigi**
Elbow	**Palkup**
Knee	**Moorup**
Back Heel	**Dwit Chook**
Head	**Mori**

Back Kick

Back Kick Foot Shape

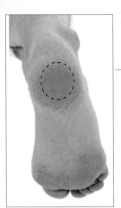

Back kick is executed using the rear sole (heel).
The back of the heel should be facing upward and
the toes facing downward, the rear sole is slightly
angled forward to strike the target.

Reverse Turning Kick

Reverse Turning Kick Foot Shape

Reverse turning kick is executed using the back
heel. The side of the foot is virtually parallel to the
ground, with the heel slightly higher than the toes.

Ibo Matsoki

Two step sparring builds on the skills developed in three step sparring. See Page 31 & 114.

Attacker

The attack begins in right L stance with forearm guarding block. The attacks will vary between each of the number sequences and use combinations of both hand and foot techniques.

Defender

The defence begins in parallel ready stance and will defend each technique with the set block or combination. The defender will use focus, distance and timing to ensure each attack is blocked effectively and the counter attack is performed with realism.

Defence and attack roles are then reversed and the sequences are repeated until requested to stop.

Number 1

Walking Stance High Obverse Punch	Walking Stance Outer Forearm Rising Block	Left Leg Front Kick	Walking Stance X Fist Pressing Block

Counter Attack

Chamber Position

Walking Stance
Twin Vertical Punch

Number 2

1

2

Fixed Stance	L Stance	Left Leg	L Stance
Side Punch	Palm Upward Block	Turning Kick	Waist Block

Counter Attack

L Stance
Side Elbow Thrust

Number 3

| Right Leg Front Snap Kick | Walking Stance X Fist Pressing Block | Walking Stance Twin Vertical Punch | Walking Stance Outer Forearm Wedging Block |

Right Leg Front Snap Kick   **Walking Stance X Fist Pressing Block**   **Walking Stance Twin Vertical Punch**   **Walking Stance Outer Forearm Wedging Block**

Counter Attack

Chamber Position

Left Leg Front Knee Kick

SAFETY NOTE
Do NOT pull opponent down towards your knee kick, release hands from shoulders and simulate striking to solar plexus.

Number 4

Walking Stance
Flat Fingertip
Thrust

Walking Stance
Knife Hand Rising
Block

Left Leg
Side Kick

L Stance
Palm Pushing
Inward Block

Counter Attack

Left Leg
Front Kick

Walking Stance
Twin Upset Punch

Ban Jayoo Matsoki
(Intermediate)

3 step semi free sparring (intermediate Level) builds on skills required for basic level.

No fixed routines are taught for this level of set sparring.

Attack

The attack begins with forearm guarding block in a right L stance.

The attacker will perform any three kicks of their choice, from front, side, turning, reverse side or back kick.

All kicks should be aimed to the middle section.

Defence

The defending student will block each kick with a waist block. The counter attack can be any hand technique, appropriate to grade.

Defender and attacker then change roles and repeat until requested to stop.

Students should kihap to notify each other that both are ready to begin. The defending student also kihaps on the counter attack.

Example Use Only

1

Turning Kick

L Stance
Waist Block

2

Front Kick

L Stance
Waist Block

3

Counter Attack

Back Kick

L Stance
Waist Block

Palm Strike

Jayoo Matsoki

Sparring is the physical application of attack and defence techniques, gained from patterns and fundamental exercises against an actual moving opponent or opponents under various situations. It is, therefore, not only indispensable to promote fighting spirit and courage, but also to forge, toughen and develop the attacking and blocking tools and to test your own skill and ability against others.

In fact, nearly all students are anxious to begin this aspect of training. This allows the student to achieve a greater degree of satisfaction through actual application of techniques. However the danger lies in a student who has not built up a solid basic foundation, developing bad habits that are extremely difficult to lose. The instructor should encourage the beginner to learn the necessary combinations and drills before participating in class sparring.

Free sparring is the sport side of Tae Kwon-Do, employing semi contact techniques in a controlled environment under instruction. Students are encouraged to try many techniques, both defence and attack. Spinning and jumping are key elements of attack, whilst dodging and avoiding to out wit your opponent is vital for effective defence.

In free sparring there is no prearranged element and both participants are completely free to attack and defend to out score each other by making contact to the permitted point scoring areas.

Hints for Sparring

Defence
Instant attack and counter attack
Deception
Selection of correct target
Direction of attack & defence
Technique experimentation
Development of tactic & manoeuvre
Dodging techniques
Flying techniques
Combination techniques
Position change

All class, grading and competition sparring in the TAGB is semi-contact. To ensure the safety of all students, they must wear a full set of safety equipment as shown below. The equipment must be TAGB approved and can be purchased through your instructor.

Sparring Foot Pads

Sparring Gloves

Head Guard

Groin Guard
(Males Only)

Gum Shield

Shin Pads

Optional
Chest Protector
(Females Only)

38 Movements

Yul Gok is the pseudonym of the great 16th century philosopher and scholar Yi I (pronounced Yee Eye) 1536 - 1584, nicknamed the Confucius of Korea. The 38 movements represent his birth place on the 38th degree line of latitude.

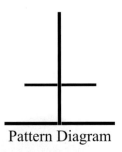

Pattern Diagram

Begin: Parallel Ready Stance

	Technique	Section	Stance	Direction
1	Left Hand Measure	Middle	S	Left slide
2	Right Punch *(FAST)*	Middle	S	-
3	Left Punch *(FAST)*	Middle	S	-
4	Right Hand Measure	Middle	S	Right slide
5	Left Punch *(FAST)*	Middle	S	-
6	Right Punch *(FAST)*	Middle	S	-
7	Inner Forearm Block	High	W	Right 45°
8	Front Snap Kick	Low	-	Foward
9	Obverse Punch *(FAST)*	Middle	W	-
10	Reverse Punch *(FAST)*	Middle	W	-
11	Inner Forearm Block	High	W	Left 90°
12	Front Snap Kick	Low	-	Forward
13	Obverse Punch *(FAST)*	Middle	W	-
14	Reverse Punch *(FAST)*	Middle	W	-
15	Obverse Hooking Block	High	W	Right 45°
16	Reverse Hooking Block	High	W	-
17	Obverse Punch	Middle	W	-
18	Obverse Hooking Block	High	W	Forward

Yul Gok Tul

	Technique	Section	Stance	Direction
19	Reverse Hooking Block	High	W	-
20	Obverse Punch	Middle	W	-
21	Obverse Punch	Middle	W	Forward
22	Forearm Guarding Block	Middle	BRS	Forward
23	Side Piercing Kick	Middle	-	Forward
24	Elbow Front Strike	Middle	W	-
25	Forearm Guarding Block	Middle	BRS	Right 180°
26	Side Piercing Kick	Middle	-	Forward
27	Elbow Front Strike	Middle	W	-
28	Twin Knife Hand Block	Mid / High	L	Left 90°
29	Straight Fingertip Thrust	Middle	W	Forward
30	Twin Knife Hand Block	Mid / High	L	Right 180°
31	Straight Fingertip Thrust	Middle	W	Forward
32	Outer Forearm Block	High	W	Left 90°
33	Reverse Punch	Middle	W	-
34	Outer Forearm Block	High	W	Forward
35	Reverse Punch	Middle	W	-
36	Back Fist Strike	High	X	Forward
37	Double Forearm Block	High	W	Right 270°
38	Double Forearm Block	High	W	Left 180°

38th Parallel

The 38th Degree line of latitude was also chosen as the division between North and South Korea. This line was decided between US and Russian troops and was only ever intended as a temporary split. The division still exists today and although no real fighting has taken place for decades, the countries are still officially at war.

Blue Belt Terminology

Blue belt signifies the Heaven, towards which the plant matures into a towering tree as training in Tae Kwon-Do progresses.

What is Korean for 2 step sparring?
Ibo Matsoki

When was Tae Kwon-Do International inaugurated?
13th November 1993

Give a brief history of the TAGB?
See page 3

50 -50 weight distribution
Toes and heels touching

Closed Ready Stance B
Moa Junbi Sogi B

1 shoulder width long between little toes. Most of the weight is on the rear leg, ball of front foot lightly touches the ground.

Rear Foot Stance
Dwit Bal Sogi

1 shoulder width wide between centre of insteps

2 shoulder widths long between big toes

Low Stance
Nachua Sogi
50 - 50 weight distribution

Palm Pressing Block
Sonbadak Noollo Makgi
Blocking Tool: Palm

Twin Straight Forearm Checking Block
Sang Sun Palmok Momchau Makgi
Block Tool: Outer Forearm

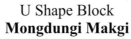

U Shape Block
Mongdungi Makgi
Blocking Tool: Reverse Knife Hand
Used to block a pole or staff, arc hand used to trap
the pole and turn block into a grab.

81

Palm Waist Block
Sonbadak Hori Makgi
Blocking Tool: Palm

X Fist Rising Block
Kyocha Joomuk Chookyo Makgi
Blocking Tool: Back of Forearms

Reverse Knife Hand Outward Block
Sonkal Dung Bakaero Makgi
Blocking Tool: Reverse Knife Hand

Palm Upward Block
Sonbadak Ollyo Makgi
Blocking Tool: Palm

Twin Upset Punch	**Sang Dwijibo Jirugi**
Twin Vertical Punch	**Sang Sewo Jirugi**
Back Fist Side Strike	**Dung Joomuk Yop Taerigi**
Side Punch	**Yop Jirugi**
Turning Punch	**Dollyo Jirugi**
Reverse Knife Hand Strike	**Sonkal Dung Taerigi**
Side Fist Strike	**Yop Joomuk Taerigi**
Flat Fingertip Thrust	**Opun Sonkut Tulgi**

Arc Hand Strike
Bandal Son Taerigi
Strike Tool: Arc Hand
Target Area: Throat

Palm Strike
Sonbadak Taerigi
Strike Tool: Palm
Target areas: Nose,
Philtrum, Chin or
Solar plexus

Elbow must pass the chin level to be effective.

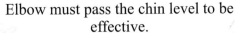

Upper Elbow Strike
Wi Palkup Taerigi
Strike Tool: Elbow
Target Area: Under Chin

Front Snap Kick
Ap Cha Busigi
Strike Tool: Ball of Foot
Target Area: Knee

Turning Punch
Dollyo Jirugi
Strike Tool: Fore Fist
Target Area: Chest / Sternum

Back Fist Side Strike
Dung Joomuk Yop Taerigi
Strike Tool: Back Fist
Target Area: Temple

The release move is performed by twisting and pulling your forearm clockwise in a downward arc.

Release Move
Jap Yasol Tae

Reverse High Punch
Bandae Nopunde Jirugi
Strike Tool: Fore Fist
Target Area: Nose / Chin

Number 5

1

Chamber Position

Right Leg
Middle Section
Reverse Side Kick

L Stance
Palm Waist Bloc

2

Counter Attack

Walking Stance
High Section
Palm Strike

L Stance
Outer Forearm Inward
Block

Walking Stance
Middle Section
Reverse Knife Hand
Strike

Number 6

| Right Leg
High Section
Turning Kick | Sitting Stance
Twin Straight Outer
Forearm Checking
Block | Walking Stance
High Section
Arc Hand Strike | L Stance
Hooking Block
& Grab |

Counter Attack

Left Leg
Middle Section
Side Kick

Number 7

L Stance
Middle Section
Side Fist Strike

L Stance
Twin Outer
Forearm Block

Left Leg
Middle Section
Reverse Turning
Kick

L Stance
Forearm
Guarding Block

Counter Attack

Right Leg
High Section
Reverse Turning Kick

88

Number 8

Right Leg
Middle Section
Side Kick

L Stance
Inner Forearm
Inward Waist Block

Chamber Position

Counter Attack

2

L Stance
High Section
Spinning Knife
Hand Strike

L Stance
Knife Hand
Guarding Block

X Stance
High Section
Back Fist Side Strike

Ban Jayoo Matsoki
(Advanced)

3 step semi free sparring (Advanced Level) builds on the skills required for intermediate level.

No fixed routines are taught for this level of set sparring.

Attack

The attack begins in forearm guarding block in L stance.
The attacker will perform three hand or foot techniques of their choice.
Any combination is allowed.

Defence

The defender will use an appropriate block or avoiding manoeuvre against each technique.
The counter attack can be any hand or foot technique appropriate to the attack. Jumping or spinning techniques can be used.

Defender and attacker then change roles and repeat until requested to stop.

With each subsequent attack, the student may begin with either left or right L stance.

Choice of technique is left to student, but the technique and skill level should be commensurate with grade.
No jumping or flying techniques are allowed on the attack phase.
Students should kihap to notify each other that both are ready to begin. The defending student also kihaps on the counter attack.

Example Use Only

1

Middle Section
Obverse Punch

Middle Section
Outer Forearm
Inward Block

2

High Section
Turning Kick

High Section
Knife Hand Block

Counter Attack

High Section
Reverse Knife Hand Strike

High Section
Knife Hand Block
Middle Section Reverse Punch

91

32 Movements

Joon Gun is named after the patriot An Joong Gun who assassinated the first Japanese Governor General of Korea, Hiro Bumi Ito. The 32 movements represent Mr An's age when he was executed in Lui Shung prison in 1910.

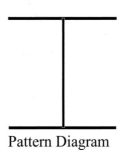

Pattern Diagram

Begin : Closed Ready Stance 'B'

	Technique	Section	Stance	Direction
1	Reverse Knife Hand Block	Middle	L	Left 90°
2	Front Snap Kick	Low	-	-
3	Palm Upward Block	Middle	RFS	Forward
4	Reverse Knife Hand Block	Middle	L	Right 180°
5	Front Snap Kick	Low	-	-
6	Palm Upward Block	Middle	RFS	Forward
7	Knife Hand Guarding Block	Middle	L	Left 90°
8	Upper Elbow Strike	High	W	-
9	Knife Hand Guarding Block	Middle	L	Forward
10	Upper Elbow Strike	High	W	-
11	Twin Vertical Punch	High	W	Forward
12	Twin Upset Punch	Middle	W	Forward
13	X fist Rising Block	High	W	Left 180°
14	Back Fist Side Strike *(FAST)*	High	L	Left 90°
15	Release From Grab *(FAST)*	Middle	W	-
16	Reverse Punch	High	W	-
17	Back Fist Side Strike *(FAST)*	High	L	Right 180°

	Technique	Section	Stance	Direction
18	Release From Grab *(FAST)*	Middle	W	-
19	Reverse Punch	High	W	-
20	Double Forearm Block	High	W	Left 90°/ Fwd
21	Side Punch	Middle	L	-
22	Side Piercing Kick	Middle	-	Forward
23	Double Forearm Block	High	W	-
24	Side Punch	Middle	L	-
25	Side Piercing Kick	Middle	-	Forward
26	Forearm Guarding Block	Middle	L	-
27	Palm Pressing Block *(SLOW)*	Mid / Low	LOW	Forward
28	Forearm Guarding Block	Middle	L	Forward
29	Palm Pressing Block *(SLOW)*	Mid / Low	LOW	Forward
30	Turning Punch *(SLOW)*	Middle	C	Left 90°
31	U-shape Block	Mid / High	F	Forward
32	U-shape Block	Mid / High	F	Foot to Foot Left 180°

Hiro Bumi Ito

Japanese statesman. Born to a samurai's adopted son, Ito received samurai status in 1863 and was sent to England to study. He rose quickly through Japanese government departments including Junior Councillor in charge of foreign affairs, Home Minister and after extensive study in Europe, became Prime Minister of the first cabinet government in 1885. In 1903, he began annexation of Korea, becoming first resident Governor General there in 1906 and in 1907 forcing the Korean sovereign's abdication. He resigned in 1909, but was assassinated at Harbin train station in Manchuria by Korean nationalist An Joong Gun.

Joon Gun Tul

Red Tag Belt Terminology

Red belt signifies danger, cautioning the student to exercise control and warning the opponent to beware.

What is Korean for 1 step sparring?   **Ilbo Matsoki**

Who are the founder members of the TAGB and what are their positions on the committee?

Mr David Oliver	**Chairman**
Mr Michael Dew	**Vice Chairman**
Mr Ron Sergiew	**Treasurer**
Mr Paul Donnelly	**Liaison Officer**
Mr Kenny Walton	**Team Coach**

In which area is your club situated?	**Ask your instructor**
Who is your area representative?	**Ask your instructor**
Give a brief history of the TAGB?	**See page 3**

Flying	**Twimyo**
Jumping	**Twigi**

Closed Ready Stance	**Moa Junbi Sogi**
Bending Ready Stance	**Guburyo Junbi Sogi**
Fixed Stance	**Gojung Sogi**
Vertical Stance	**Soo Jik Sogi**
X Stance	**Kyocha Sogi**

Why do we jump into X stance in TOI GYE?
To avoid a stick swung beneath legs horizontal to the ground.

94

Knife Hand Low Guarding Block
Sonkal Najunde Daebi Makgi
Blocking Tool: Knife Hand

What are the two uses for circular block?
Block two separate techniques at different heights or to scoop a kick up to unbalance your opponent.

X Fist Pressing Block   **Kyocha Joomuk Noollo Makgi**
Inner Forearm Middle Block   **An Palmok Kaunde Makgi**
Palm Inward Pushing Block   **Sonbadak Anaero Miro Makgi**
Inner Forearm Circular Block   **An Palmok Dollimyo Makgi**

Posture position for
W shape block

Outer Forearm W Shape Block
Bakat Palmok San Makgi
Blocking Tool: Outer Forearm

Double Forearm Pushing Block
Doo Palmok Miro Makgi
Blocking Tool: Inner Forearm

X Fist Pressing Block
Kyocha Joomuk Noollo Makgi
Blocking Tool: Back of Forearms
Used to block a front kick or knee kick.

Back Fist Strike &
Outer Forearm Low Block
**Dung Joomuk Taerigi & Bakat
Palmok Najunde Makgi**
Strike Tool: Back Fist
Blocking Tool: Outer Forearm
Technique shown in closed stance & L stance.

Upset Fingertip Thrust
Dwijibun Sonkut Tulgi
Strike Tool: Fingertips
Target Area: Groin

Flat Fingertip Thrust	**Opun Sonkut Tulgi**
Side Punch	**Yop Jirugi**
Twin Vertical Punch	**Sang Sewo Jirugi**
Knife Hand Inward Strike	**Sonkal Anaero Taerigi**
Knee Kick	**Moorup Chagi**
Back Kick	**Dwit Chagi**
Head	**Mori**
Waist	**Hori**

Ilbo Matsoki

One step sparring has no set routines.
This is the most realistic form of set sparring and closest to a real self defence situation.

The defence against attack is down to the students choice and their application of technique and skill. A greater application of focus, distance, timing, speed and reaction is required to create effective techniques.

Attack

The attacker begins in parallel ready stance and following a kihap, steps forward with right walking stance middle section obverse punch.

Defence

The defender will then use a series of techniques to block and counter-attack against the attacker.

The same attack and defence is then repeated on the left side.

Techniques should reflect the grade and skill level. Focus, distance and timing are crucial for safe and competent execution.

Jumping and spinning techniques are encouraged.

See Page 31 & 114.

Example 1

Knife Hand Block   Reverse Punch

Example 2

Forearm Guarding Block   Jumping Front Kick

37 Movements

Toi Gye is the pen name of the 16th Century scholar Yi Wang who was regarded as an authority on neo-confucianism. The 37 movements represent his birth place on the 37th degree latitude.
The diagram represents the calligraphy for scholar.

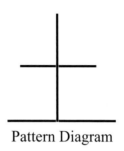

Pattern Diagram

Begin: Closed Ready Stance 'B'

	Technique	Section	Stance	Direction
1	Inner Forearm Block	Middle	L	Left 90º
2	Upset Fingertip Thrust	Low	W	-
3	Back Fist Strike /	High	C	Right 90º
	Outer Forearm Low Block *(SLOW)*	Low	C	-
4	Inner Forearm Block	Middle	L	Right 90º
5	Upset Fingertip Thrust	Low	W	-
6	Back Fist Strike /	High	C	Left 90º
	Outer Forearm Low Block *(SLOW)*	Low	C	-
7	X Fist Pressing Block *(CONT)*	Low	W	Forward
8	Twin Vertical Punch *(CONT)*	High	W	-
9	Front Kick	Middle	-	Forward
10	Obverse Punch	Middle	W	-
11	Reverse Punch	Middle	W	-
12	Posture Move *(SLOW)*	-	C	Left 90º
13	W Shape Block *(STAMPING)*	High	S	Left 90º
14	W Shape Block *(STAMPING)*	High	S	Right 180º
15	W Shape Block *(STAMPING)*	High	S	Right 180º
16	W Shape Block *(STAMPING)*	High	S	Left 180º
17	W Shape Block *(STAMPING)*	High	S	Right 180º

Toi Gye Tul

Technique	Section	Stance	Direction
W Shape Block *(STAMPING)*	High	S	Right 180º
Dbl Forearm Pushing Block	Low	L	Forward
Grab to Shoulders	High	W	-
Knee Kick	Middle	-	-
Knife Hand Guarding Block	Middle	L	Left 180º
Front Snap Kick	Low	-	-
Flat Fingertip Thrust	High	W	-
Knife Hand Guarding Block	Middle	L	Forward
Front Snap Kick	Low	-	-
Flat Fingertip Thrust	High	W	-
Back Fist Strike /	High	L	Backwards
Outer Forearm Low Block	Low	L	-
X Fist Pressing Block	Low	X	Jump Forward / Left 90º
Double Forearm Block	High	W	Right 90º
Knife Hand Guarding Block	Low	L	Left 270º
Inner Forearm Circular Block *(RIGHT)*	Middle	W	-
Knife Hand Guarding Block	Low	L	Right 180º
Inner Forearm Circular Block *(LEFT)*	Middle	W	-
Inner Forearm Circular Block *(RIGHT)*	Middle	W	-
Inner Forearm Circular Block *(LEFT)*	Middle	W	-
Right Punch	Middle	S	Left 90º

eo-Confucianism

eo Confucianism refers not to a new
nterpretation of the ancient
onfucianism but a renewed interest in
e traditional teachings. The movement
entred on intellectual and spiritual
rowth, ultimately leading to ultimate
ersonal fulfilment. Neo Confucianism
pread quickly throughout East Asia and
ill today is a cornerstone of
hilosophical teachings in western
ociety.

The symbol for Neo Confucianism

101

Red Belt Terminology

Red belt signifies danger, cautioning the student to exercise control and warning the opponent to beware.

1 step sparring	**Ilbo Matsoki**
2 step sparring	**Ibo Matsoki**
3 step sparring	**Sambo Matsoki**
3 step semi free sparring	**Ban Jayoo Matsoki**
Free sparring	**Jayoo Matsoki**

What is the difference between 1, 2 and 3 step sparring?

Use of focus, distance & timing become vital as the complexity of technique increases. The student needs to look to the tenets of Tae Kwon-Do and exercise self control, in addition to adding an element of realism. The complexity of attack is increased from punching to hand and foot combination techniques. The use of speed and reaction also adds the element of realism to the set sparring. (See Page 31 & 114)

Who is your area representative?	**Ask your instructor**
Why are there 24 patterns?	**See page 12**
How do we develop power in a pattern?	**See page 12**

What is the difference between a STRIKE and a THRUST?

A strike is designed to smash or destroy the target area and can impact from any angle to either soft or hard targets.

A thrust is designed to penetrate the target area and only drives straight towards the soft areas of the body.

Which patterns have a release move in them?
Do San, Joon Gun & Hwa Rang.

Give a brief history of Tae Kwon-Do?	**See page 6**
Give a brief history of the TAGB?	**See page 3**

Closed Ready Stance 'C'
Moa Junbi Sogi 'C'

Palm Pushing Block
Sonbadak Miro Makgi
Blocking Tool: Palm

Sitting Stance	**Annun Sogi**
L Stance	**Niunja Sogi**
Vertical Stance	**Soo Jik Sogi**
Walking Stance	**Gunnun Sogi**

Outer Forearm Low Block
Bakat Palmok Najunde Makgi
Inner Forearm Middle Block
An Palmok Kaunde Makgi

Upward Punch
Ollyo Jirugi
Strike Tool: Fore Fist
Target Area: Solar Plexus / Jaw

(L Stance) Obverse Punch
Baro Jirugi
Strike Tool: Fore Fist
Target Area: Solar Plexus

Knife Hand Downward Strike
Sonkal Naeryo Taerigi
Strike Tool: Knife Hand
Target Area: Collar Bone

Side Elbow Thrust
Yop Palkup Tulgi
Strike Tool: Elbow
Target Area: Solar Plexus / Ribs

Release Move from Hwa Rang
Jap Yasol Tae

Side Piercing Kick
Yop Cha Jirugi
Strike Tool: Foot Sword
Target Area: Solar Plexus

Close up of release grasp.

The grasping hand in the release move should be placed around the front knuckles of the punching arm. The release and side piercing kick are performed as a combination technique.

Double Punch
Knife Hand Strike
Straight Fingertip Thrust
Upper Elbow Strike

Doo Jirugi
Sonkal Taerigi
Son Sonkut Tulgi
Wi Palkup Taerigi

Downward Kick
Naeryo Chagi
Strike Tool: Back Heel

Crescent Kick
Bandal Chagi
Blocking Tool: Sole / Reverse Foot Sword

Hooking Kick
Golcho Chagi
Strike Tool: Back Heel

Reverse Turning Kick
Bandae Dollyo Chagi
Strike Tool: Back Heel

Flying Side Kick
Twimyo Yop Chagi
Strike Tool: Foot Sword

Turning Kick
Front Snap Kick
Flying Kick
Back Kick
Side Piercing Kick
Reverse Hook Kick

Dollyo Chagi
Ap Cha Busigi
Twimyo Chagi
Dwit Chagi
Yop Cha Jirugi
Bandae Dollyo Goro Chagi

29 Movements

Hwa Rang is the name given to an army of young warriors from the Silla Dynasty of Korea. They were first mentioned in AD 600, and over the years they gradually became a significant force in the unification of Korea's three kingdoms.

Hwa Rang means "Flowering Youth", and comprises of 29 movements which refer to the 29th Infantry Division where Tae Kwon-Do developed.

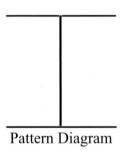

Pattern Diagram

Begin: Closed Ready Stance 'C'

	Technique	Section	Stance	Direction
1	Palm Pushing Block	Middle	S	Left Slide
2	Double Punch	Middle	S	-
3	Twin Outer Forearm Block	High / Mid	L	Right 90°
4	Upward Punch	High	L	-
5	Sliding Side Punch	Middle	F	Right Slide
6	Knife Hand Downward Strike	High	V	-
7	Obverse Punch	Middle	W	Forward
8	Outer Forearm Block	Low	W	Left 90°
9	Obverse Punch	Middle	W	Forward
10	Release From Grab	-	W	-
11	Side Piercing Kick	Middle	-	Forward
12	Knife Hand Strike	Middle	L	-
13	Obverse Punch	Middle	W	Forward
14	Obverse Punch	Middle	W	Forward

	Technique	Section	Stance	Direction
15	Knife Hand Guarding Block	Middle	L	Left 270°
16	Straight Fingertip Thrust	Middle	W	Forward
17	Knife Hand Guarding Block	Middle	L	Left 180°
18	Turning Kick	High	-	Forward
19	Turning Kick	High	-	Forward
20	Outer Forearm Block	Low	W	Left 90°
21	Obverse Punch	Middle	L	-
22	Obverse Punch	Middle	L	Forward
23	Obverse Punch	Middle	L	Forward
24	X Fist Pressing Block	Low	W	-
25	Side Elbow Thrust	Middle	L	Forward
26	Inner Forearm Block /	Middle /	C	Left 90°
	Outer Forearm Block	Low	C	-
27	Inner Forearm Block /	Middle /	C	-
	Outer Forearm Block	Low	C	-
28	Knife Hand Guarding Block	Middle	L	Forward
29	Knife Hand Guarding Block	Middle	L	Right 180°

Hwa Rang

The Hwa Rang were a group of young men who were both highly educated and expertly trained. They studied from a very young age, mastering many forms of military combat, but also focusing on the arts and literature.

The Hwa Rang were noted for their horsemanship as well as the array of weapons they used, including unarmed combat. They specialized in battle tactics and many of these have been used by modern armies, allowing small numbers to attack and overcome a larger force.

The Hwa Rang often led the Silla army into battle, and rarely lost.

Black Tag Belt Terminology

Black is the opposite of white, signifying maturity and proficiency in Tae Kwon-Do. Also indicates the wearers imperviousness to darkness and fear.

Name ALL the stances that you know? (English & Korean)

X Knife Hand Checking Block	Twin Palm Upward Block
Kyocha Sonkal Momchau Makgi	**Sang Sonbadak Ollyo Makgi**
Blocking Tool: Knife Hand	Blocking Tool: Palm

Knife Hand Guarding Block	**Sonkal Daebi Makgi**
Outer Forearm Low Block	**Bakat Palmok Najunde Makgi**
Forearm Guarding Block	**Palmok Daebi Makgi**
U Shape Block	**Mongdungi Makgi**
Double Forearm Block	**Doo Palmok Makgi**
Outer Forearm Front Block	**Bakat Palmok Ap Makgi**
Forearm Rising Block	**Palmok Chookyo Makgi**

Reverse Knife Hand Inward Strike
Sonkal Dung Anaero Taerigi
Strike Tool: Reverse Knife Hand
Target Area: Neck

Knife Hand Inward Strike
Sonkal Anaero Taerigi
Strike Tool: Knife Hand
Target Area: Neck

NOTE
Hand under elbow is
acting as a guard.

NOTE
Hand in front of forehead is a guard
against a close up attack.

Flat Fingertip Thrust   **Opun Sonkut Tulgi**
Straight Fingertip Thrust   **Son Sonkut Tulgi**
Upset Fingertip Thrust   **Dwijibun Sonkut Tulgi**
Back Fist Strike   **Dung Joomuk Taerigi**
Back Fist Side Strike   **Dung Joomuk Yop Taerigi**
Reverse Punch   **Bandae Jirugi**
Back Fist Rear Strike   **Dung Joomuk Dwitcha Taerigi**

Outer Forearm Middle Inward Block
Bakat Palmok Kaunde Anaero Makgi
Blocking Tool: Outer Forearm

Chamber Position
Back Fist Side Strike

Back Fist High Side Strike
Dung Joomuk Nopunde Yop Taerigi
Strike Tool: Back Fist
Target Area: Nose

U Shape Block
Mondungi Makgi
Blocking Tool: Reverse Knife Hand

The technique is performed by jumping simultaneously with both feet, whilst rotating 360 degrees. The take off stance is fixed stance and the landing is in L stance. The take off and landing are on the same spot.

The purpose of this 360 degree jumping spin is to disorientate the opponent.

Knife Hand Guarding Block
Sonkal Daebi Makgi
Blocking Tool: Knife Hand

Matsoki

Set Sparring

Students at this grade and subsequent dan grades can be requested to perform any of the set sparring learnt previously.
Performance should be commensurate with their grade.
Emphasis on focus, distance and timing is coupled with an increase of speed, power and accuracy. Students should develop an element of realism into the formal set of exercises.

Semi Free Sparring

Students at this grade and subsequent grades can be requested to perform 3 step semi free sparring during their grading. Unless instructed otherwise the student will perform the advanced form of this sparring.
The student should show a complete understanding of the attack and defence techniques used, and ensure they are competent to perform these to the best of their ability.
Students are encouraged to use jumping techniques in their counter attack, whilst still exercising control and accuracy.

Free Sparring

Students at this grade and subsequent grades will be requested to spar 3 separate bouts against various opponents.
The student should be able to demonstrate control, speed, footwork, defence and attack techniques.
The student must also understand how the use of a good guard and dodging techniques can be used to win the fight.
A student will also be judged on their tactics against different opponents; it is vital to be able to adapt to various heights, weights, abilities and sexes.

Your in depth knowledge of Tae Kwon-Do

General Questions
Name all the hand parts and / or foot parts?
Name all the target areas on the high / middle / low sections?

Name all the kicks you know?
Name all the finger tip thrusts, knife hand techniques or punches you know?
What is Taek Kyon?

Pattern Interpretation
Explain why Choong Moo finishes in a left hand technique and what is meant by unrestrained potentiality?

Pattern Movements
Which three patterns have a release move (Jap Yasol Tae) in them?
What is the purpose of X stance?

Further information - Patterns
What is a Kobukson?
What have Yul Gok and Toi Gye got in common?

You and Tae Kwon-Do
Which other martial arts have influenced Tae Kwon-Do?
Why do we learn the meanings of patterns?
What have you gained from Tae Kwon-Do?
Why should the TAGB award you a black belt?
What have you done to deserve a black belt?
What qualities should a black belt possess?
What qualities does your instructor have that you would like to emulate?

NOTE
The answers to these questions have been intentionally left out as they require the student training towards their black belt to take the time to look deeper in to the art and find out about the history and the tradition of Tae Kwon-Do. These are only examples of types of questions you may be asked. At this grade you may be asked any questions contained in this book.

In Depth

30 Movements

Choong-Moo was the name given to the Yi Dynasty Admiral Yi Sun-Sin. In AD1592, he was reputed to have invented the worlds first armoured battleship (Kobukson), which is said to be the precursor of today's submarine. The reason the pattern ends with a left hand attack is to symbolize his regrettable death, having no chance to show his unrestrained potentiality checked by the forced reservation of his loyalty to the king.

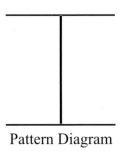

Pattern Diagram

Begin: Parallel Ready Stance

	Technique	Section	Stance	Direction
1	Twin Knife Hand Block	High / Mid	L	Left 90°
2	Guard / Inward Knife Hand Strike	High	W	Forward
3	Knife Hand Guarding Block	Middle	L	Right 180°
4	Flat Fingertip Thrust	High	W	Forward
5	Knife Hand Guarding Block	Middle	L	Left 90°
6	Forearm Guarding Block	-	BRS	Right 180°
7	Side Piercing Kick to rear	Middle	-	Forward
8	Knife Hand Guarding Block	Middle	L	Left 180°
9	Flying Side Piercing Kick	High	-	Forward
	Knife Hand Guarding Block	Middle	L	-
10	Outer Forearm Block	Low	L	Left 270°
11	Grab (opponents head)	High	W	Forward
12	Knee Kick	Middle	-	-
13	Reverse Knife Hand Strike	High	W	Left 180°
14	Turning Kick	High	-	Forward
15	Reverse Side Kick	Middle	-	Backward
16	Forearm Guarding Block	Middle	L	Right 180°

	Technique	Section	Stance	Direction
17	Turning Kick	Middle	-	To 45° Diag.
18	U-shape Block	High / Mid	F	Right 135°
19	Jump turn 360°	-	-	Left 360°
	Knife Hand Guarding Block	Middle	L	-
20	Upset Fingertip Thrust	Low	W	Forward
21	Back Fist Strike /	High	L	Backward
	Outer Forearm Low Block	Low	L	-
22	Straight Fingertip Thrust	Middle	W	Forward
23	Double Forearm Block	High	W	Left 270°
24	Front Outer Forearm Block	Middle	S	Left 90°
	Back Fist Side Strike	High	S	-
25	Side Piercing Kick	Middle	-	Left 90°
26	Side Piercing Kick	Middle	-	Forward
27	X Knife Hand Checking Block	Middle	L	Right 135°
28	Twin Upward Palm Block	Middle	W	Forward
29	Forearm Rising Block	High	W	Right 180°
30	Reverse Punch	Middle	W	-

Kobukson

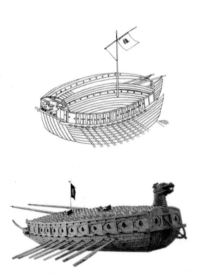

The Kobukson, also known as the Turtle Ship, was the first ironclad warship in the world, first used around 1592.

The ship was unparalleled in terms of firepower and mobility, boasting numerous cannons and even flame throwers. It proved instrumental in achieving victory in the sea battles under Admiral Yi. Described as a sea tank, it was capable of sinking large numbers of enemy vessels, and so did much to maintain the morale of Korean sailors, so often outnumbered by the vast fleets of the Japanese navy.

A replica of a Kobukson can be found in the British Maritime Museum.

Hand Parts - Sang Basin

Hand
Son

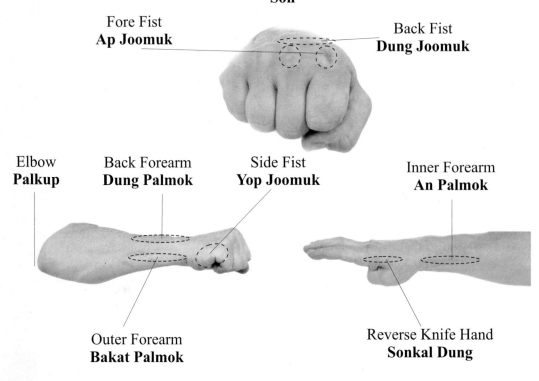

Fore Fist
Ap Joomuk

Back Fist
Dung Joomuk

Elbow
Palkup

Back Forearm
Dung Palmok

Side Fist
Yop Joomuk

Inner Forearm
An Palmok

Outer Forearm
Bakat Palmok

Reverse Knife Hand
Sonkal Dung

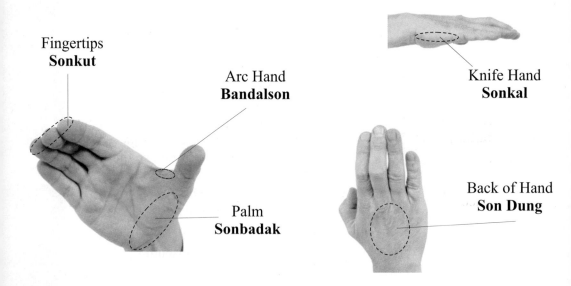

Fingertips
Sonkut

Arc Hand
Bandalson

Knife Hand
Sonkal

Palm
Sonbadak

Back of Hand
Son Dung

Foot Parts - Ha Basin
Foot
Bal

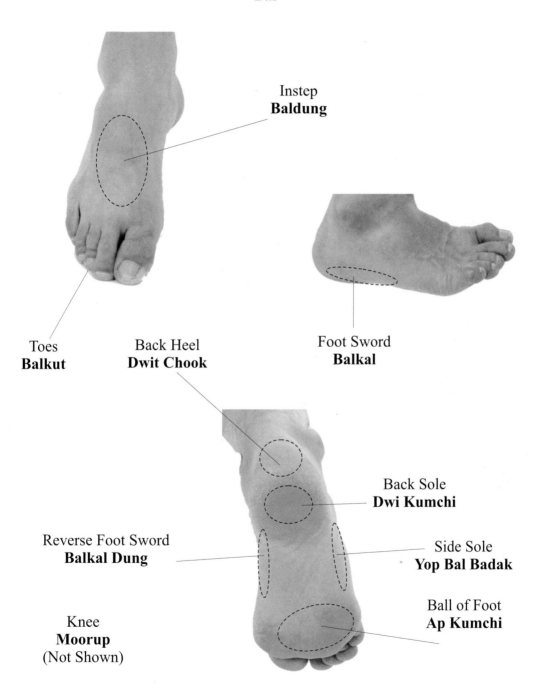

Instep
Baldung

Toes
Balkut

Back Heel
Dwit Chook

Foot Sword
Balkal

Back Sole
Dwi Kumchi

Reverse Foot Sword
Balkal Dung

Side Sole
Yop Bal Badak

Ball of Foot
Ap Kumchi

Knee
Moorup
(Not Shown)

Front Target Areas

HIGH

MIDDLE

LOW

Nose
Kotdung

Bridge of Nose
Migan

Eyes
Angoo

Temple
Gwanja Nori

Philtrum
Injung

Jaw
Yop Tok

Chin
Mit Tok

Carotid Artery
Mok Dongmaek

Neck
Mok

Collar Bone
Swe Gol

Solar Plexus
Myong Chi

Windpipe
Soom Tong

Wrists
Son Mok

Abdomen
Bokboo

Floating Ribs
Nuk Gol

Groin
Sataguni

Scrotum
Nang Shim

Inner Thigh
Anjok Hobok
Dari

Knee Joint
Moorup Gwanjol

Shins
Jong Kwaeng-I

Ankle
Balmok

Toes
Balkut

NOTE
The Korean word for joint is Gwanjol, this applies to all body joints such as the wrist, knees, ankles, etc

120

Rear Target Areas

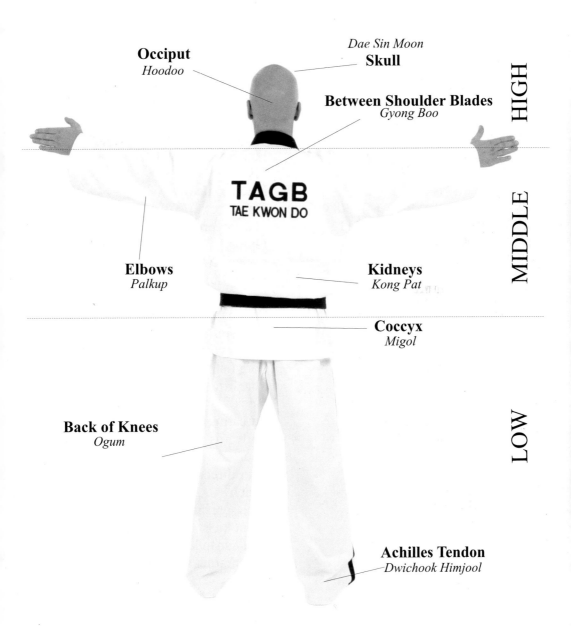

Occiput
Hoodoo

Dae Sin Moon
Skull

Between Shoulder Blades
Gyong Boo

HIGH

Elbows
Palkup

Kidneys
Kong Pat

MIDDLE

Coccyx
Migol

Back of Knees
Ogum

LOW

Achilles Tendon
Dwichook Himjool

Index - English

123

Index - Korean

127